The Vegan Ch

Ditching Dairy Has Never Been Easier

Riki Berko

The information in this book is designed for educational purposes only. It is not intended to be a substitute for informed medical advice or care. You should not use this information to diagnose or treat any health problems or illnesses without consulting your pediatrician or family doctor. Please consult a doctor with any questions or concerns you might have regarding your condition.

ISBN: 1508587965

ISBN-13: 978-1508587965

DEDICATION:

This book is dedicated to those who will never rest until they achieve their goals. To the ones that are aiming to create the best version of themselves. To all the open minded people out there. To the ones that are willing to open their heart and listen, and to all of those people that are being criticized everyday for the way that they live or the road that they have chosen. Never ever settle. People may hate you for being different and not living by society's standards, but deep down, they wish they had the courage to do the same!

Free E-books Club:

I would like to give you a full access to my VIP club in which you receive FREE E-books on a weekly basis:

Receive Free E-books Here:

http://bit.ly/150k24J

I do this simply because I want my readers to get a lot of value, reach their maximum potential and have a better life. Be the change you want to see in the world!

There is another gift waiting for you at the end of the book.

Other Recommended Books:

Table of Contents

Introduction

One of the biggest complaints my vegan friends have about their choice of vegan diet is that they miss cheese. They miss having cheese on their pizza, toasted cheese sandwiches, and cheese in pastas amongst other cheesy delights.

This got me thinking. There must be a recipe book that gives easy recipes for vegan cheese. I searched and searched, but found nothing that had recipes that were simple to make and used every day ingredients.

This is how this recipe book came about. Being vegan is a lifestyle choice taken because people don't want to consume animal products, damaging chemicals or hormones that are round in our every day food stuffs. It is a choice for a healthy, balanced diet, which is kind on the body and also on the animals that share this beautiful planet with us.

I hope that this recipe book brings you much happiness as you work your way through the many cheese recipes and add them to your daily diet. I have tried to add as many different varieties as I can, and kept the writing friendly and conversational, so that you feel as if you have a fellow vegan with you as you create your cheesy masterpieces.

Garlic and Herb Vegan Cheese

Ingredients:
1 1\2 cups of soya milk or other vegan milk
1 teaspoon crushed garlic
1 teaspoon mixed herbs - dried
1 – 1\2 teaspoons cornstarch
3 teaspoons agar flakes
1\4 teaspoon salt
4 teaspoon yeast flakes – optional as it is tasty without it too.

Method:
1. Bring 1 cup of the milk, the herbs and the garlic to the boil. This will infuse the milk with the flavor.

2. When it is boiling nicely, remove it from heat.

3. Put the corn starch and the agar flakes into the other 1\2 cup of milk and mix well, making sure it dissolves completely.

4. I have found that using a mixture of agar and cornstarch together makes for a creamier cheese.

5. When you have a nice smooth consistency, add it to the hot milk and stir well.

6. When it thickens, remove from the heat and put it in a suitable container.

7. Refrigerate to allow it to set.

Vegan mozzarella cheese

Ingredients -
- 1 Cup unsweetened soy yogurt (Another option: vegan yogurt recipe, see below)
- Cup cashew soaked for 3-8 hours
- Glass of water (divided into two halves)
- 1.5 teaspoons of sea salt
- 3 tablespoons of tapioca flour
- 1 tablespoon of agar-agar powder (or 2-3 tablespoons of Agar-agar flakes – you can grind the flakes to make a powder in a spice grinder)

Preparation:
1. Put in a blender: the yogurt, cashews, half a cup of water and salt and mix until you get a smooth, creamy texture.

2. Transfer to a large bowl and leave aside to rest with a towel placed over. The towel should not really seal the air just rest lightly.

3. Leave to rest for about 12-24 hours for fermentation of the batter in order to get the special taste of the mozzarella cheese.

4. Shuffle in the tapioca flour.

5. Now let's take care of the agar-agar:
In a pot, mix the Agar-agar with half glass of plain water, let it boil and reduce the heat and leave it for another 3-4 minutes.

6. Add the batter to the pot and then mix well for a few minutes until the texture is smooth, shiny and a little solid.

7. Fill a large bowl with water and ice cubes. Create little balls while using 2 tablespoons and place them in the cold bowl.

8. Leave the Mozzarella balls in the cold water for 20-30 minutes and it is ready to be eaten.

Vegan Yogurt

Ingredients:

300 milligrams sugar free soy milk

2-4 probiotic bacteria capsules which can be emptied and can have their contents released into the milk. (can be purchased in pharmacies)

Directions:

1. It is important that every vessel that comes into contact with the milk is sterilized in boiling water.

2. If this is stable soy milk, there is no need to sterilize anything and it is enough just to heat it to fifty degrees Celsius. If this is not stable soy milk, boil it and then bring it to fifty degrees.

3. Pour ½ cup of soy milk (heated to 50 degrees) into a small bowl, add a capsule of probiotics, and stir well to dissolve all of the bacteria. Then stir in the rest of the milk.

4. Keep the bowl at a temperature of 45 degrees Celsius (not more, because higher temperatures will kill the bacteria).

5. In order to keep the heat, you can simply keep the bowl in the oven with the lowest temperature possible or you can keep the bowl in a picnic box with a few hot water bottles.

6. The yogurt will be ready in 12-18 hours. Next time, you can take a half cup of the previously made yogurt instead of the bacteria (keep in a sterile, closed container).

Vegan Halloumi Cheese

Ingredients:
100g natural cashews soaked in water, preferably several hours
150 ml of fresh water
1 package (300 g) of soft tofu (wipe the liquids and cut for the blender (see the note below)
3 tablespoons lemon juice
Tablespoon of brewer's yeast flakes - it gives a strong cheese flavor but it is optional –
alternatively you can add a little more **granulated garlic** / garlic flakes
Tablespoon olive oil
About 1/2 teaspoon salt
About -1/2 teaspoon **granulated garlic**
Ground black pepper
1/2 teaspoon light miso - gives saltiness and a strong flavor - – alternatively you can replace with
a small amount of soy sauce
1 Tablespoon rice flour (Sticky Brown rice flour)

Before preparation - soak cashews and water before preparing in order for the cashews to be soft
and easily grind in the blender, preferably at least 4 hours. You can soak them for a longer time in
a closed container in the refrigerator.

Preparation:

1. Drain and rinse the cashews from the soaking water. Grind in a blender the cashew and the fresh
    water in order to create as smooth cashew cream as possible.
2. Add the remaining ingredients and blend in a blender until you get a smooth puree (as smooth as
    possible), taste and adjust the seasoning if needed.
3. Grease a baking pan with olive oil.
    With a 20X30 cm baking pan, you will receive slices of "cheese" of almost 1 cm thickness), Spread
    the batter inside the baking pan and bake at 180 degrees until starting to get a light brown color.
4. Cool (preferably cool in the refrigerator), at this point it is possible to cut into cubes of about 1X1
    cm and use it as a salty cheese for salad. The second option is to cut into rectangles in the size of
    halloumi cheese slices.
5. Before serving, fry the slices lightly with olive oil until golden and serve.

Vegan Cottage Cheese

Ingredients for cottage cheese:
*⅔ cup homemade cashew milk/cream

400 grams hard tofu (only hard)

**½ cup vegan mayonnaise

*Ingredients for the Cashew milk:
½ cup cashews (raw, not roasted or salted)

2 cups sugar-free soymilk (or other plant milk with a neutral flavor)

Preparation for the cashew milk/cream:
Soak the cashews in the same container as the soymilk and keep them in the fridge for at least eight hours.

Transfer to a blender and smash/blend well until the mixture is as smooth as possible. Use a cloth to strain the cheese-- it is possible to strain it with a strainer underneath. Strain the milk until it is able to through the fabric entirely and a small part of what is not ground/processed well is left.

**Ingredients for the Vegan mayonnaise:

½ cup unsweetened soymilk

1 cup grapeseed/canola/safflower oil

2 teaspoon salt

½ teaspoon mustard (you can use powder if you wish)

2 tablespoons lemon juice

¼ teaspoon apple cider vinegar

Preparation for the Vegan mayonnaise:

Put all the ingredients except the lemon in a food processor (blender) and blend, gradually adding the lemon until the mixture looks perfect.

Preparation for the cottage cheese:

After preparing the mayonnaise and cashew milk, all that remains is to mix the ingredients.

Take the tofu out of the liquid in its packaging, and squeeze it well, as much as you can. Crush it lightly with the cheesecloth, since it absorbs the liquid well.

Using a fork or your hands (I prefer using my hands directly), crumble the tofu into tiny crumbs, mix the tofu with the mayonnaise and cashew milk and add a little salt/lemon juice to taste. Transfer it to the fridge in an airtight container so it can absorb the flavor.

The tofu should absorb the flavors from the liquids. If it turns out a bit dry, add a bit of cashew milk/cream.

Vegan Parmesan

Ingredients:

1 cup cashews (dry or roasted)

½ cup nutritional yeast flakes (you can find them under the name "brewer's yeast" in stores)

2 tablespoons pine nuts

¾ teaspoon salt

¼ teaspoon garlic powder

pinch of cardamom

pinch of English pepper (optional)

Directions:

1. Put all of the ingredients in a food processor and grind/process until you get a finely ground mixture.

2. Put in an airtight/sealed container in the fridge and keep for about 3-4 weeks.

Basic Vegan Gouda Cheese

Gouda is a mild cheese with a rubbery texture. It is not high in cheesy flavor, and good for people who don't like the strong flavor of cheddar or mold cheese.

Ingredients:
1 1\2 cups soya milk
4 teaspoons agar
3 teaspoons corn starch to thicken the cheese
1\4 cup of soya milk
1 teaspoon Tumeric for colour
1\4 teaspoon salt

Method:

1. Bring 1 cup of the milk to the boil
2. When it is boiling mix the agar powder to the other milk making sure there are no lumps and you have mixed it well.
3. Add it to the milk and turn the heat down.
4. Let it simmer until all the agar granules have dissolved.
5. Add the 1\4 cup of milk to the cornstarch and mix it until you have a smooth paste.
6. Add some of the hot milk to the cornstarch and mix well.
   This is to avoid adding the cold milk to the hot milk and making lumps.
7. Add the turmeric and stir again, you can add more turmeric to adjust the colour. It just depends on how yellow you want your cheese to be. You can also leave out the turmeric and have a white cheese.
8. Add the salt.
9. Transfer the cheese to a shallow dish.
10. Refrigerate for an hour or so.

This cheese does not melt nicely and should be used for sandwiches, salads and curries, or soups.

Vegan Macadamia Cheese

Ingredients:

80 grams macadamia nuts
20 grams cashews
2 cloves of garlic
a sprig of fresh rosemary and oregano (mine are picked fresh from the garden; allow me to brag a little)
juice of half a lemon
water (enough until you reach the desired thickness)
salt to taste

Directions:

1. Put all the ingredients in a blender and blend until you reach the consistency of paste.

There is no need to soak the nuts. If your blender is not powerful enough or you have doubts about it, it is possible to soak them and facilitate the process. 2-3 hours in water is enough.

Zucchini vegan cheese spread

Ingredients:
1 cup peeled and sliced zucchini (also known as baby marrows)
Enough water to cover zucchini
1 tablespoon olive oil
1 tablespoon vinegar
1 flat teaspoon agar powder
2 tablespoons nutritional yeast
Pinch of sea salt

Method:
1. Boil the peeled zucchini in the water until very tender.
2. Drain well or your cheese will be watery.
3. Mash the zucchini and return to the pot.
4. Sprinkle the agar powder over the mash and stir very well and quickly or the agar will make lumps.
5. When it is smooth and well mixed, add the other ingredients
6. Cook over a love heat for about 5 minutes until it becomes firmer.
7. Don't let it catch on the bottom.
8. Add more salt if desired.
9. Transfer to a bowl and refrigerate for at least an hour.

Vegan Yoghurt Cottage Cheese

Ingredients:

2 cups of vegan yoghurt – plain but a high fat content if possible.
1 – 2 teaspoons vinegar
1\4 teaspoon salt
Muslin or fine mesh cloth
Sieve

Method:

1. Bring the yoghurt to the boil.
2. Watch it and keep stirring as it burns easily.
3. When it is boiling nicely, remove it from heat.
4. Add the vinegar to the yoghurt, don't stir it, and allow it to split naturally.
5. Yoghurt doesn't split like milk does, so your curds will be smaller than when making paneer or tofu.
6. Once you have some clear liquid and some curds, remove from the heat.
7. Put your cloth into your sieve and place it over a bowl
8. Pour the mixture into the cloth and stir it gently.
9. Leave it to drain, just go and scrape down the cheese off the edges from time to time.
10. When most of the liquid has drained through, close the cloth around the cheese and squeeze the remaining liquid from the cheese. You cannot be too strong otherwise all your cheese is just going to escape through the material.
11. When it feels as if most of the liquid has been removed, twist the top of the cloth and place the cheese ball, still in the cloth, in the refrigerator to set.
12. After about 1\2 hour, remove from the refrigerator and gently open the cloth. The cottage cheese will not be totally set, and this is how it is meant to be.

Serve in salads, on crackers, toast or on top of pizza.

Potted Cranberry Cheese

Ingredients:
1 Cup soya milk or any vegan milk alternative.
2 teaspoons agar powder
6 teaspoons yeast flakes
1\4 teaspoon salt

Method:
1. Bring the milk to the boil.
2. When it is boiled, remove from heat.
3. Sprinkle the agar powder over the milk froth and stir like crazy.
4. When you are sure you don't have any lumps, add the yeast flakes and the salt.
5. Remove from the heat and add the cranberries.
6. Put it in a suitable bowl and allow to cool and set.

This is delicious with crackers and preserved figs

Vegan "Safed" Cheese

Ingredients:

1 cup cashews (soaked for at least one hour)

¼ cup water

tablespoon lemon juice

2 teaspoons Himalayan salt

½ teaspoon black pepper

1 tablespoon agar-agar and 1 cup water

20 chopped olives/ hyssop-Za'atar (and many more options)-- optional

Directions:

1. Grind the cashews in the blender with the ¼ cup water, the lemon juice and the spices.
2. Bring to a boil, stirring, and add 1 cup water as well as 1 tablespoon agar-agar.
3. Pour the water with the agar into the blender and mix just until you get a smooth mixture.
4. Transfer to a bowl and stir 20 chopped olives into the cheese or secure them to the bottom of the silicone mold (alternatively, you can add hyssop and Nigella to the cheese, as well as many other options). Another option is to transfer half of the cheese to a baking dish, mold over the olives (as a middle layer) and above another layer of cheese.
5. Refrigerate for 12 hours (to stabilize).

Smoked Paprika Vegan Soft Cheese

Ingredients:
1 1\2 cups plain vegan yoghurt
1\4 cup of soya milk or another vegan milk.
1 1\2 teaspoons smoked paprika
1 – 1\2 teaspoons cornstarch
1\4 teaspoon salt
4 teaspoon yeast flakes

Method:
1. Bring the yoghurt to the boil, stirring continuously.
2. When it is boiling nicely, remove it from heat.
3. Put the corn starch and the yeast flakes along with the salt and paprika into the other 1\2 cup of milk and mix well, making sure it dissolves completely.
4. When you have a nice smooth consistency, add it to the hot milk and stir well.
5. When it thickens, remove from the heat and put it in a suitable container.
6. Refrigerate to allow it to cool.

This is a soft cheese, so it will not set, but has a lovely smooth and creamy consistency.

Basic Paneer recipe

Ingredients:
1\2 gallon vegan milk, or equivalent such as almond milk
Vinegar or lemon juice.
Colander
Muslin cloth

Method:
1. Place your muslin cloth in your colander over a bowl. Make sure that you can have both your hands free, and don't need to hold the colander.

2. Warm milk and as it boils and froths, add the vinegar – around 1\5 – 1\4 of a cup. I use vinegar as the lemons I get are not always acidic enough and the milk does not split. I also vary the amount, and try and use as little as possible so that there is no aftertaste of vinegar to the cheese.
So if you try it, and your milk remains together, add a little vinegar. The best thing is that you don't taste the vinegar in the cheese.

3. As soon as the milk splits properly, so that you have lumps of curds and a discernible watery whey – strain the liquid from the curds through your muslin cloth.

4. Scrape the sides of the cloth so that all the curds are together in the middle of the cloth.

5. Twist the cloth and as it starts cooling, twist again to make it as tight as you can.

6. Place something heavy on the tightly closed cloth to force the rest of the liquid out.

7. Refrigerate the cheese whilst still in the cloth until you can feel that the cheese has hardened.
Open it gently and remove your cheese round.

There you have it – your own paneer!

Sweet Paneer

Ingredients:
1 1\2 cups of vegan yoghurt - plain
¼ cup of soya or other vegan milk
1 – 1\2 teaspoons vinegar

Method:
1. Bring the yoghurt to the boil.
2. Watch it and keep stirring as it burns easily.
3. When it is boiling nicely, remove it from heat.
4. Put in the vinegar and it will immediately split.
5. Pour the mixture into the cloth that you have put into a sieve and push all the water out.
6. Twist the cloth to get all the liquid (whey) out.
7. As you drain the basic paneer, stir in cranberries, molasses or treacle.
8. Put it in a suitable container.
9. Allow to cool in the refrigerator

It can be served with strawberries, preserved fig, in fruit salad or with crisp green apples for a delicious after dinner dessert.

Vegan Herb Smoked Cheese

Ingredients:
1 1\2 cups of soya milk
4 teaspoons agar powder
4 teaspoons corn starch
1\4 cup nutritional yeast – more if you want a very cheesy flavor
1 teaspoon of mixed herbs
Turmeric for coloring

Method:
1. Heat 1 cup of the milk in a saucepan until it boils
2. Add the agar powder and the starch to the other cold 1\2 cup of milk
3. Add the agar mixture to the hot milk and stir well
4. Cook on a low heat for 5-7 minutes
5. Add the nutritional yeast and stir again until the mixture thickens
6. Transfer to a baking pan or glass dish and refrigerate for at least an hour.

Cashew cheese

Ingredients:
1 cup natural cashews
water
juice of half a lemon
1 tablespoon extra virgin olive oil
salt to taste

Directions:
1. Soak cashews in a bowl with a lot of water for 4-8 hours at room temperature.
2. Drain and rinse the cashews, then put them in a blender.
3. Add a quantity of water that is in height equivalent to ⅓ of the height of the cashews in the blender, the lemon juice, and the oil.
4. Blend until you reach the consistency of cheese.
5. Taste and add salt and lemon if necessary.

Can be kept several days refrigerated in a closed jar.

Alternatives(optional):
You can add garlic, fried onions, olives.

You can add a handful of herbs to taste like basil, hyssop, parsley or dill.

You can add more or less water to the mixture according to personal taste.

Vegan Herb Gouda Cheese

Ingredients:

1 1\2 cups soya milk
5 teaspoons agar powder
1 teaspoon white vinegar
4 teaspoons corn starch
1 teaspoon smoked paprika
1 teaspoon mixed green herbs or origanum
1 teaspoon turmeric for coloring – more can be added if necessary
Nutritional yeast flakes can be added to make the cheesy flavor stronger. Start with 1\4 cup and add to taste.

Method:
1. Heat 1 cup of milk in a pot until it boils
2. Mix the other ingredients together with the other 1\2 cup of cold milk
3. Pour the hot milk into the cold liquid mixture
4. Return to the heat and stir over a lower heat until all the agar granules have dissolved.
5. Transfer to a bread tin or a baking dish
6. Allow to cool and use in sandwiches or as a snack.

Vegan Yoghurt Cream Cheese

Ingredients:
1 1\2 cups of vegan yoghurt - plain
¼ cup of soya or other vegan milk
1 – 1\2 teaspoons cornstarch
1\4 teaspoon salt
1 teaspoon yeast flakes – optional as it is tasty without it too.

Method:
1. Bring the yoghurt to the boil.
2. Watch it and keep stirring as it burns easily.
3. When it is boiling nicely, remove it from heat.
4. Put the corn starch into the milk and mix well, making sure it dissolves completely.
5. When you are sure you don't have any lumps, add the yeast flakes and the salt.
6. Return to the heat and stir well.
7. If the mixture becomes too thick, add a little more milk.
8. You want a spreadable, but smooth, creamy consistency.
9. Put it in a suitable bowl and allow to cool .

This is delicious on bagels.

Almond Feta Cheese

Ingredients:

145 grams ground almonds (you can grind them, but I bought them already ground and weighed, so I didn't have to get involved in the weighing process)

½ cup water

¼ cup fresh lemon juice

3 tablespoons olive oil

1 clove of garlic (in my opinion, that's more than enough)

1 ¼ teaspoon salt

Directions:

1. Place all the ingredients in a food processor and grind until the mixture becomes a paste.

2. Transfer the mixture to cloth "diapers" (*I cannot think of a better way to put it*)/ "squeeze bags" or gauze "diapers" and tie the top. Wait until you get the desired round shape.

3. Put the cloth in a sieve, and the sieve on top of the bowl and put it in the fridge for 12 hours.
   Note: In practice, if you use a bit less water in advance, 2-3 hours in the fridge are enough.

4. After cooling the cheese, heat the oven to 180 degrees and prepare a non-stick mold or bowl in which to bake the cheese. Take the cheese out of the fridge, undo the tie, open the fabric, and put the cheese into the baking pan so that the pretty, smooth side is on top.

5. Bake the cheese uncovered for about 40 minutes or until the top starts to brown. It is supposed to split open from the top during baking.

Tofu Cheese Spread

Ingredients:
1 1\2 cups soya milk
2 tablespoons vinegar – use as much a needed or as little as needed to split the milk
1\4 teaspoon salt
1 sieve
Muslin cloth or other fine meshed cloth to drain the cheese through.

- This has got to be the easiest cheese recipe I have ever made. You can add whatever spices you like to make different spreads.

Method:
1. Bring 1 cup of the milk to the boil.
2. When it is boiling, add the salt and remove from heat.
3. Add 1 tablespoon vinegar.
4. Lay the cloth in the sieve.
5. When the cheese has split transfer it to the cloth and drain it well.
6. The mixture is hot, so take care not to burn yourself. Rather wait a minute or so for it to cool before you squeeze out as much liquid as you can.
7. Transfer it to a dish and refrigerate for about half an hour.

Almond Cheese

Ingredients:

1 cup of peeled and soaked almonds (roughly 200 grams soaked in water for 12 hours)

To quickly and easily peel almonds, soak them in boiling water for ten minutes and then the shell can be removed easily.

¾ cup of water

⅓ cup of drained lemon juice

one level teaspoon of salt

4 cups of olive oil

2 cloves of garlic (to taste)

Directions:

1. Put the shelled almonds in the food processor and grind well. Mix from time to time to get a uniform texture.

2. Add the rest of the ingredients.

3. Continue grinding and mixing until you get a uniform mixture.

Spicy yellow vegan cheese with herbs

Ingredients:

Part One:

200 grams cashews
½ teaspoon salt (5 grams)
65 ml oil for you to choose (olive oil is not preferable because of its strong taste)
70 gram of brewer's yeast flakes
½ teaspoon turmeric
½ teaspoon garlic powder
3 tablespoons sweet white miso
300 milliliters water
½ teaspoon Tabasco sauce
½ teaspoon dried parsley flakes
½ teaspoon dried cilantro flakes

Part Two:

To dissolve the agar-agar:
200 milliliters water
6 tablespoons agar-agar flakes or 3 tablespoons agar-agar powder
a little oil (to grease the pan)
½ teaspoon cilantro flakes or parsley or any dried spice that you want (for decoration)

Directions:

1. Blend the ingredients in part one in a blender/food processor until the mixture becomes uniform.
2. Melt the agar-agar in water over medium heat for about five minutes until the agar has melted and the sauce seems thick.

3. Mix the melted agar-agar in a food processor together with the rest of the ingredients.

4. Grease the baking pan, sprinkle some herbs at the bottom, pour the mixture on top, cover and refrigerate for several hours the cheese becomes solid.

Vegan Yoghurt Cheese

Ingredients:
1 cup vegan yoghurt
2 teaspoons agar powder
1\4 teaspoon salt
Yeast flakes to takes – optional
An egg whisk or fork
Recipes can be double and even tripled should you want a larger quantity of cheese.

Method:
Bring the yoghurt to the boil, stirring continuously.
When it boils remove it from heat.
Sprinkle the agar powder over the milk froth and stir like crazy using the egg whisk or a fork if you don't have a whisk.
Keep whisking the mixture whilst you return it to the heat.
When it thickens, take it off the heat and give it another good whisk.
This is going to make it light and fluffy and full of little air pockets.
Put it in a bowl and place it in the refrigerator to cool.
Turn it out when it is cool and admire the lovely texture of your mild cheese.

Vegan Olive Cheese Spread

Ingredients:
Regular **Tofutti** cheese
Pitted olives
Black pepper
Nutmeg
Cinnamon and cardamom

Directions:
Put all the ingredients into a food processor or spice grinder and grind/process until you reach a uniform texture. It can be refrigerated for up to seven days.

Yellow Cheese For Pizzas/Toast

Ingredients (for 8 slices (one family pizza):
1 cup of sugar-free soy milk
¾ teaspoon salt
1 level teaspoon brewer's yeast powder
½ teaspoon light miso
1 heaping tablespoon flour (wheat or white)
1 teaspoon corn flour (cornstarch)
Pinch of turmeric (just a little!)
3 tablespoons olive oil
1 teaspoon of **Agar Agar powder** - not less than 4
grams! (Or 3 tablespoons **Agar flakes**, see comments
below)

Preparation:

1. Scramble well all ingredients in a pot, let it boil while scrambling vigorously, and cook over medium heat for 2-3 minutes.
2. Remove from the fire, to devour little.
3. Pad tray with plastic wrap and flatten the mixture with a spatula until it becomes one sheet.
4. Cover with plastic wrap and refrigerate 30 minutes.
5. Cut the surface to 8 rectangles, store refrigerated while separating each slice with plastic wrap between slices.

Notes:
* The miso and the **nutritional yeast** can be replaced with other spices according to personal taste: garlic powder, tomato sauce, etc.
* Giving up on the Agar Agar powder is not recommended. I use the powder because it works better than the flakes. Since you can buy the Agar in both forms, in order for the recipe to succeed in crystallizing, use a teaspoon of Agar powder or 3 teaspoons of Agar flakes (you should melt the flakes in half the amount of soy milk, cook and devour well until complete dissolution - 5 minutes at least. Scramble the flour and other ingredients into half a cup of soy milk and add to the mixture of the Agar flakes for 3 minutes more. It is easier to just buy agar powder). The Agar can be found in health food stores, shops and specialty spices stores for baking.
* The cheese does not create "wires" but it melts nicely for pizza and toast and it has a rich, creamy texture after dissolution.
* You can keep the cheese in the refrigerator for about a week.
* For those who are sensitive to Soy, you can be prepare the cheese from Cashew Milk, made by grinding a handful of cashews in a glass of water and continue the recipe as usual.

Balsamic Paneer

Ingredients:
2 cups vegan milk
2\3 teaspoons balsamic vinegar
Good pinch of salt.
A fine meshed cloth such a muslin.
A sieve

Method:
1. Heat the milk in a pan on the stove with the added salt.
2. As soon as it boils and froths, add the balsamic vinegar,
3. It will immediately split, the curds being the solid parts and the whey being the liquid.
4. Put the cloth in the sieve and rest it on a suitable bowl so that it is properly balanced.
5. Pour the mixture into the cloth and push the liquid out using the back of a serving spoon or wooden spoon.
6. When there is no more liquid coming out, twist the cloth around the mixture and wring it out some more. Make sure you don't burn yourself on the hot water.
7. Put the cheese into the refrigerator in the cloth to set.
8. After about half an hour, you can remove your paneer and cut it into blocks to use.

Vegan Cheese Spread

Ingredients:

1 ¼ cups of peeled and soaked almonds (they must be soaked for at least 8 hours)

¾ cup of soaked of cashews (they must be soaked for at least 2 hours)

4-5 tablespoons lemon juice

½ teaspoon of salt (add to taste)

1 clove of garlic

¼-⅓ cup of water

Directions:

1. Put the almonds and cashews into the blender together with the lemon, water, garlic and spices and blend until you get a smooth texture. (It is preferable to use a stronger blender setting so as to get a smoother texture.)

2. If the texture is too thick, you can gradually add water while mixing until you reach the desired texture.

3. Transfer the cheese to a glass container and put it in the fridge, where it can be kept for up to one week.

Note: for those who are interested in a "cheesier" taste, you can add 2-3 tablespoons of brewer's yeast to strengthen/enhance the taste.

Onion and Herb Vegan Yoghurt Cheese

Ingredients:

1 1\2 cups of vegan yoghurt
¼ cup soya milk
2 teaspoons agar powder
6 teaspoons yeast flakes
1\4 teaspoon salt
1 teaspoon onion flakes
1 teaspoon garlic flakes
1\2 teaspoon mustard
Pinch of paprika
Pinch of tumeric

Method:

1. Bring the yoghurt to the boil.
2. With yoghurt you have to keep an eye on it as it burns very quickly.
3. When it is boiling remove it from heat.
4. Sprinkle the agar powder into the milk and mix well.
5. Add the cold milk and agar mixture to the hot yoghurt and keep stirring
6. When you are sure you don't have any lumps, add the other ingredients.
7. Mix well.
8. When it begins to thicken, remove it from the heat.
9. Put it in a suitable bowl and allow to cool and set.

White Vegan Cheese

This is a mild white cheese, and can be used in salads, for sandwiches or pastas.

Ingredients:
1 1\2 cups soya milk
4 teaspoons agar
3 teaspoons corn starch to thicken the cheese
1\4 cup of soya milk
1\4 teaspoon salt

Method:
1. Bring 1 cup of the milk to the boil
2. When it is boiling mix the agar powder to the other milk making sure there are no lumps and you have mixed it well.
3. Add it to the milk and turn the heat down.
4. Let it simmer until all the agar granules have dissolved.
5. Add the 1\4 cup of milk to the cornstarch and mix it until you have a smooth paste.
6. Add some of the hot milk to the cornstarch and mix well.
7. This is to avoid adding the cold milk to the hot milk and making lumps.
8. Add the salt
9. Transfer the cheese to a shallow dish.
10. Refrigerate for an hour or so.

Soft cream cheese

Ingredients:
1 1\4 cup of soy milk or other vegan milk
2 teaspoons cornstarch
1\4 teaspoon salt
4 teaspoon yeast flakes

Method:
1. Bring the milk to the boil, stirring continuously.
2. When it is boiling nicely, remove it from heat.
3. Put the corn starch and the yeast flakes along with the salt into the other 1\4 cup of milk and mix well, making sure it dissolves completely.
4. When you have a nice smooth consistency, add it to the hot milk and stir well.
5. When it thickens, remove from the heat and put it in a suitable container.
6. Refrigerate to allow it to cool.
7. This is a spreading, so it will not set, but, like the paprika cheese, it has a lovely smooth and creamy consistency.

If you want to use it for dipping, just warm it a little and it will become runny again.

Baked Almond Vegan Feta Cheese

Ingredients:

145 grams ground, peeled almonds (you can buy them pre-ground, so there is no need to soak them)-- it's about ½ cup or 100g peeled almonds which are soaked for about 5 hours
45 grams cashews soaked for about 5 hours
60 grams lemon juice (¼ cup)
½ cup of water
3 tablespoons olive oil
2 cloves garlic, crushed
¼ teaspoon of salt

Directions:

1. Put all the ingredients in a food processor/blender and grind/blend until the texture becomes creamy.

2. Use a small bowl, sieve, and cloth "diaper" for the cheese. Arrange the cloth over the strainer and the strainer over the bowl.

3. Pour all the batter from the blender into the cloth that is resting on top of the strainer on the bowl.

4. Collect all the corners of the cloth and tie them with a rubber band. Transfer to the refrigerator for about 12 hours. You can also just leave it for the night and bake the next day.

5. Take the cheese out after 12 hours. You can use the same heat-proof bowl to bake the cheese, but make sure to wipe it down a bit (there may be residual water at the bottom of the cheese). Lubricate it with a little spray or dab with olive oil and wipe with paper towels.

6. Put the cheese in the bowl with the top down, so that we get a smooth cheese ball.

7. Bake at 180 degrees for 40 minutes or until it reaches a beautiful golden color and the cheese is slightly cracked on top.

8. Spread the olive oil mixture on top.

Fresh Pepper Paneer spread with herbs

Ingredients:
1 1\2 cups of vegan yoghurt - plain
¼ cup of soya or other vegan milk
1 – 1\2 teaspoons vinegar
1 small onion
Half a red pepper
Half a yellow pepper

Method:
1. Fry your onion and peppers until soft.
2. Bring the yoghurt to the boil.
3. Watch it and keep stirring as it burns easily.
4. When it is boiling nicely, remove it from heat.
5. Add your onions and peppers.
6. Put in the vinegar and it will immediately split.
7. Pour the mixture into the cloth that you have put into a sieve and push all the water out.
8. Twist the cloth to get all the liquid (whey) out.
9. Put it in a suitable container
10. Allow to cool in the refrigerator.

Cheesy cheese sauce

Ingredients:
1 1\2 cups soya milk
1 – 1 1\2 teaspoons cornstarch
1 teaspoon vegan butter equivalent (optional)
2 tablespoons yeast flakes – the more you add the stronger the cheesy flavor will be
1\2 teaspoon mustard
Pinch of salt

Method:
1. Bring 1 cup of the milk to the boil.
2. When it is boiling, add the salt and remove from heat.
3. Add the half cup of cold milk to the cornstarch and stir well. There should be no lumps.
4. Add the cornstarch milk mixture to the hot milk and mix well.
5. It will thicken immediately.
6. Should it still look a little runny add a little more milk\cornstarch mixture but remember that it is a pouring sauce so you don't want it to set.
7. Add the yeast and mustard and stir again.

Your sauce is ready for use.

Vegan Soy Cheese

Ingredients:

2 liters of sugar-free soy milk (Alpro with the red label)
3 medium size lemons
3/4 cup boiling water
To taste:
Salt
2 cloves of garlic
You will need a strainer, cloth for making cheese, a bowl, a large pot with a lid, a spoon for mixing and a blender / food processor.

Directions:

1. Turn on the kettle to heat the water needed.

2. Arrange the bowl as shown: above it, the strainer and on it, the cloth for the cheesemaking.

3. Pour the 2 liters of soymilk into a big pot and heat until the water begins to simmer. Turn off the heat.

4. Squeeze the lemons into a glass with the ¾ of the boiling water then mix. Pour a third of the lemon with the water into the pot with the milk and then mix.

5. After about five minutes, add a little bit and then mix. After another five minutes, add the rest, cover for a few minutes and you can already see how the milk slowly reacts - gets a cheesy texture in the pot.

6. After a maximum of fifteen minutes, the cheese has separated enough from the water in the pot and it is alright to move it into a colander that is already prepared with a bowl and cloth. Fluid will drip into the bowl. It is also possible to squeeze the cheese slightly by tightening the cloth, but you do not want it too dry. You definitely do not want it too wet, so what you can do is wring it thoroughly, and when you transfer it to a blender, add a little water from the amount that was squeezed that is still in the bowl, if necessary. The water will be slightly yellowish.

7. In the blender, add the garlic and salt, grind everything and, if necessary, add more water until it reaches the desirable texture and softness appear and the cheese is ready for use.

Notes:

- It can be kept in the fridge for a week as is.
- If you want it to have the texture of ricotta cheese, do not add the water and do not grind it. Just crumble slightly with a fork and season with what you love.

Vegan Basil Pesto Cheese

Ingredients:
 1 cup vegan yoghurt
1 cup plain yoghurt
1 teaspoon vegan mayonnaise (optional)
3 teaspoons agar powder
1\4 teaspoon salt

Method:
1. Bring the yoghurt and the milk to the boil, stirring continuously.
2. When it boils remove it from heat.
3. Sprinkle the agar powder over the milk froth and stir continuously to avoid getting lumps.
4. When it is smooth, return it to the heat.
5. Stir until it begins to set.
6. Take if from the heat and add the basil pesto.
7. When it thickens, take it off the heat and give it another good whisk.
8. Put it in a bowl and place it in the refrigerator to cool.

This is a very pretty cheese and would be good in pasta.
NB: Nut allergy sufferers should note that pesto has pine nuts in it.

Chilli chilli Cheese

Ingredients:
1 1\2 cups of soya milk or any vegan milk alternative – go for one that has a high fat content.
2 teaspoons agar powder
3 teaspoons yeast flakes
1\4 teaspoon salt
 1\4 Chili flakes – more if you are brave enough.
Pinch of turmeric for colour
1 teaspoon of smoked paprika

Method:
1. Bring the milk to the boil.
2. When it is remove from heat.
3. Sprinkle the agar powder over the milk froth and stir well.
4. Make sure you don't put it back on the heat until all the agar has dissolved.
5. Add the rest of the ingredients and stir again.
6. Put it back on the heat and stir gently until the mixture starts to thicken
7. Put it in a suitable bowl and allow to cool and set.
8. This one has a real sharp bite, so if you don't like hot food, halve the amount of chilies.

Conclusion

Now that we have come to the end of our cheese making journey together, I hope that you have had as much fun making the cheeses as I did putting the recipe book together. I believe in the vegan way of life, and my wish is that everyone can see that there is always a vegan option for whatever you want to eat. Learning to live as one with the earth and all its creatures in the most harmonious way to live, and eating pure, good, healthy and tasty food is a wonderful part of that way of living.
Enjoy and happy cheese making!

Finally, if you enjoyed this book, please take the time to share your thoughts and post a review on Amazon.
It'd be greatly appreciated!

Thank you and good luck!

Recommended Books

Below you'll find some of my other popular books that are popular on Amazon and Kindle as well. Simply click on the links below to check them out. Alternatively, you can visit my author page on Amazon to see other work done by me.

Everything That Used To Have Eggs, Is Now Vegan: Don't Give Up Your Favourite Recipes Only Because It Has Eggs

Vegan Kids Box Set: Vegan Recipes For Kids & Vegan Diet For Kids

Build Muscle on the Raw Vegan Diet: How to Gain Muscle Mass and Stay Fit on the Raw Food Diet

Everything That Used To Have Meat, Is Now Vegan: Don't Give Up Your Favourite Recipes Only Because It Has Meat

Everything That Used To Have Fish, Is Now Vegan: Don't Give Up Your Favourite Recipes Only Because It Has Fish

Everything That Used To Have Cheese, Is Now Vegan: Don't Give Up Your Favorite Recipes Only Because It Has Cheese

Food Addiction: How To Develop Self Discipline, Control Your Eating And Overcome Food Addiction

If the links do not work, for whatever reason, you can simply search for these titles on the Amazon website to find them.

27735073R00030

Made in the USA
Middletown, DE
20 December 2015